To:
Aiden

Dec.
2022

Love F

MW01015716

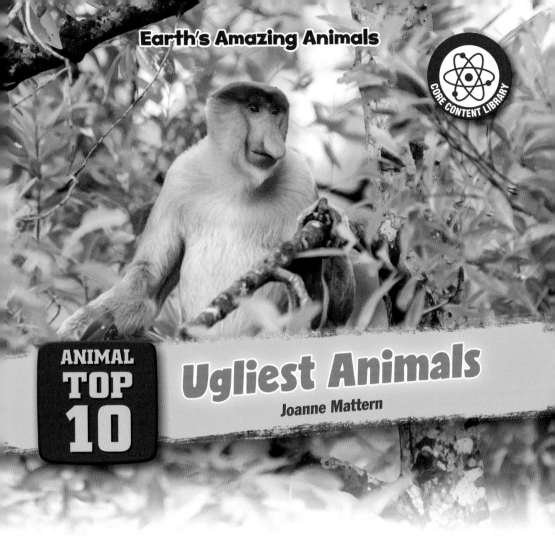

CORE CONTENT LIBRARY

ANIMAL
TOP
10

Ugliest Animals

Joanne Mattern

RED
CHAIR
·PRESS·

Earth's Amazing Animals is produced and published by Red Chair Press:

Red Chair Press LLC   PO Box 333   South Egremont, MA 01258-0333

www.redchairpress.com

Publisher's Cataloging-in-Publication Data
Names: Mattern, Joanne, 1963–
Title: Animal top 10. Ugliest animals / Joanne Mattern.
Other Titles: Animal top ten. Ugliest animals | Ugliest animals | Core
content library.

Description: South Egremont, MA : Red Chair Press, [2019] | Series:
    Earth's amazing animals | Includes glossary, Power Word science term
    etymology, fact and trivia sidebars. | Interest age level: 007-010. |
    Includes bibliographical references and index. | Summary: "Which
    animal's head is shaped like a shovel and covered in bumps? Did you
    know two animals have wiggly worm-like flesh to attract prey? Some
    animals are pretty ugly!"--Provided by publisher.

Identifiers: LCCN 2018955616 | ISBN 9781634406925 (library hardcover) |
    ISBN 9781634407885 (paperback) | ISBN 9781634406987 (ebook)

Subjects: LCSH: Morphology (Animals)--Juvenile literature. | Ugliness--
    Juvenile literature. | Animals--Juvenile literature. | CYAC: Morphology
    (Animals) | Ugliness. | Animals.

Classification: LCC QL799.3 .M38 2019 (print) | LCC QL799.3 (ebook) |
    DDC 591.4/1--dc23

Copyright © 2020 Red Chair Press LLC

RED CHAIR PRESS, the RED CHAIR and associated logos are registered
trademarks of Red Chair Press LLC.

All rights reserved. No part of this book may be reproduced, stored in an
information or retrieval system, or transmitted in any form by any means,
electronic, mechanical including photocopying, recording, or otherwise
without the prior written permission from the Publisher. For permissions,
contact info@redchairpress.com

Illustrations by Tim Haggerty.

Map illustration by Joe LeMonnier.

Photo credits: cover (top), pp. 3, 5 (top, bottom), 6–9, 17–21, 37 (top right),
38, 39 iStock; cover (bottom), pp. 1, 5 (center), 10, 13–15, 22, 25, 37 (bottom
left) Shutterstock; p. 11 © Dembinsky Photo Ass./Minden Pictures; p. 27
© Frans Lanting Studio/Alamy; p. 29 © Kyodo News/Getty Images; p. 30
© The History Collection/Alamy; p. 32 © Paul Fleet/Alamy; p. 33 © William
West/Getty Images; p. 34 © Barry Durrant/Getty Images; p. 36 © FLPA/
Minden Pictures; p. 37 (top left) © Kelvin Aitken/VWPics/Alamy; p. 37
(center) © Bradley van der Westhuizen/Alamy; p. 37 (bottom right) © Brian
Parker/Alamy.

Printed in United States of America

0519 1P CGF19

Table of Contents

Introduction

The world is full of beautiful animals. However, the world is also full of animals that are just plain ugly! An animal might be called ugly because it has a big nose or a huge mouth. It might be slimy or spiky. It might have a funny shape or a body that doesn't seem to have a shape at all!

Whatever the reason, there are some very strange-looking animals out there. Sometimes an animal's odd body parts actually help it find food or escape from **predators**. Other times, an animal's looks are hard to explain.

We've put together a list of the Top Ten Ugliest Animals. Take a look and see why these animals are the most unusual-looking creatures on Planet Earth!

And the Winners Are...

Here are our choices for the Top 10 Ugliest Animals. Turn the pages to find out more about each of these ugly creatures.

10. The Proboscis Monkey

9. The Vulture

8. The Star-Nosed Mole

7. The Alligator Snapping Turtle

6. The Hammerhead Shark

5. The Warthog

4. The Monkfish

3. The Naked Mole Rat

2. The Blobfish

1. The Giant Squid

#9

#7

#3

10 The Proboscis Monkey

"Proboscis" is another word for big nose. It's easy to see how this monkey got its name! A male proboscis monkey's nose can be up to 4 inches long. This nose isn't just long. It is also large and wide. The monkey's nose is so long, it hangs down below the animal's mouth.

Only male proboscis monkeys have such big noses. Scientists think they blow air through the nose to make loud noises. These big sounds help attract females. So a big nose can be a big help when a monkey is looking for a mate!

Male proboscis monkeys have the big noses.

9 The Vulture

A vulture's claim to ugliness is mostly in its head. Its head and neck have no feathers on them. The bare, pink flesh is not very nice to look at. But it helps the vulture in a big way.

Vultures are **scavengers**. They eat dead animals. The bare skin on its head and neck may help the vulture stay clean. If the bird had feathers there, they would be covered in blood and other gross stuff from the dead animals that they eat. That blood and other stuff could be filled with germs that would make the vulture sick.

Vultures are excellent at flying. Their big, strong wings mean they can glide in the air for hours.

There are many different species of vultures. Some are as tall as 3 feet (1 meter).

The Ugly Truth

Vultures live on every continent except Australia and Antarctica.

The Star-Nosed Mole

Say hello to the star-nosed mole, a wiggly-faced animal that comes in at #8 on our big-ugly list.

Star-nosed moles have almost no eyesight.

The star-nosed mole gets its name from the 22 tentacles around its hairless, pink nose. These animals live underground in wet areas. They dig through the ground looking for food. Sometimes they dive and swim in ponds.

Star-nosed moles can barely see anything. They need to feel around to find their food. Those wiggly tentacles can feel the slightest movement or object in the soil. This ability lets the star-nosed mole find insects and worms to eat in no time. Star-nosed moles can even smell underwater!

The Ugly Truth

The star-nosed mole's long, strong claws make it crazy good at digging.

7 The Alligator Snapping Turtle

Watch out! This animal is not only ugly, it is a master of destruction! This tough-looking creature looks like something from prehistoric times. However, it is alive and well today. These turtles can be found in rivers, lakes, and **canals** all over the southeastern part of the United States.

A snapping turtle's jaws really do snap! An alligator snapping turtle's jaws can snap closed so quickly, its prey has little chance of getting away. Another danger is that the turtle's jaws are very sharp. An alligator snapping turtle would have no trouble biting off someone's finger!

The Ugly Truth

Unfortunately, a loss of habitat has made alligator snapping turtles an endangered species.

Alligator snapping turtles are the largest freshwater turtles in the Western Hemisphere. One turtle that lived in an aquarium weighed 249 pounds (113 kg). In the wild, male turtles can weigh between 175 and 225 pounds (79–102 kg). Females are much smaller. They only weigh about 50 pounds (23 kg).

Some prey are fooled by the red worm-like flesh in the turtle's mouth!

Alligator snapping turtles have another trick up their ugly jaws. This turtle has a red, worm-shaped piece of flesh in its mouth. The turtle will lay on the river bottom and stick out this blob of flesh. Soon a fish or frog will swim close, thinking the flesh is actually a tasty worm. Then—snap! The turtle's jaws close around its prey, and dinner is served. Snappers will also eat snakes, raccoons, armadillos, and even other turtles. But underwater animals are the easiest to catch. An alligator snapping turtle can stay underwater for up to 50 minutes, just waiting for dinner to come too close.

6 The Hammerhead Shark

Animal heads are supposed to be round, right? Not if you are a hammerhead shark! This shark's head really does look like a hammer. Its head stretches out just like the top of a hammer. The shark's eyes are on each end of its long head. Its tooth-filled mouth is underneath.

Hammerheads might look weird, but their ugly heads help them find prey. Because this shark's eyes are so far apart, it can see in almost every direction. The shark can also move and turn very quickly. And the shape of its head lets it hold down stingrays it finds under the sandy bottom. This is good news for the shark, because stingrays are its favorite food!

The Ugly Truth

Despite their scary look, Hammerhead sharks almost never attack people.

This shark doesn't just use its eyes to find food. Its big head can also sense electrical signals that are given off by other sea creatures.

Hammerhead sharks live in oceans all over the world. They often swim near coral reefs. They also live in bays and usually swim in shallow water. These creatures can grow between 12 and 30 feet (3.5 to 9 m) long.

Hammerhead shark

5 The Warthog

The warthog will never win any beauty contests. Its head is shaped like a shovel and is covered with bumps. Long **tusks** stick out of its mouth. However, looks aren't everything. This creature is one of the smartest and strongest animals in Africa.

The warthog is smarter than it looks.

As you might guess from its name, warthogs are related to pigs. A warthog is about three to five feet (1–1.5 m) long. These animals are covered with rough hair and have manes running down their backs. But what really stands out is the warthog's head. It is narrow at the top and wide at the bottom. Its mouth has four long tusks sticking out. The upper tusks can be up to two feet (0.6 m) long. Thick bumps grow all over its head. Those bumps protect the warthog if it gets in a fight.

This creature is usually very peaceful. Instead of fighting, it will run away from predators such as cheetahs, hyenas, and lions. A warthog will jump into its underground den, rear end first! That way, their tusks stick out of the den to protect the animal. If a warthog does have to defend itself, its sharp tusks and teeth do a great job.

The Ugly Truth

A warthog can run up to 30 miles (48 km) an hour.

A happy pair

Warthogs don't need to hunt their prey. These animals are herbivores. They are happy to snack on the grass that grows all over the African savanna. These animals often roll around in the mud. A mud bath helps the warthog cool off. It also gets rid of insects that like to bite. Sometimes birds ride on top of the warthog and eat insects from its fur. This keeps both the warthog and the bird happy!

Male warthogs usually live alone. Females can live in groups of up to 40 animals. They growl, snort, and squeal to communicate with each other.

4 The Monkfish

The monkfish is not just ugly, it is scary-looking! However, its weird and frightening appearance is just what the monkfish needs to survive.

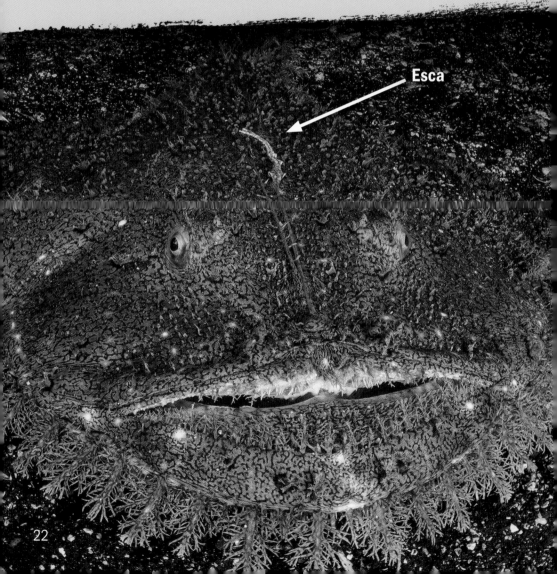

Esca

The first thing you notice about the monkfish is its mouth. This fish's mouth is the widest part of its face. The mouth is lined with rows of very sharp teeth that point in. Also, the monkfish's bottom jaw sticks out. This makes the mouth look even bigger and scarier. And the huge mouth and sharp teeth make it easy for the monkfish to grab and hold onto the fish, squid, and crabs it likes to eat.

The monkfish has other body parts that help it catch and eat its prey. This fish has a piece of flesh called the esca that sticks out of its head. The esca looks like a worm. If a fish or crab comes close to try to catch the "worm," the monkfish quickly grabs it with its big mouth and sharp teeth. Dinner is served!

Monkfish live way down in the ocean. They can live as deep as 3,000 feet (915 m) below the surface. Although they mostly eat the fish and other creatures that live deep underwater, sometimes these fish will swim to the surface. There they will grab and eat small birds that are swimming in the water.

Monkfish swim slowly. Sometimes they use their fins to walk across the bottom of the sea instead. A female can lay up to a million eggs during one season. When the eggs hatch, the tiny larvae stay near the top of the water. When they are about three inches (8 cm) long, they start swimming down to their home on the bottom of the sea.

Monkfish might look ugly, but they taste good! Many people in Europe and the United States enjoy eating this fish. However, only some parts of the fish are good to eat.

The Ugly Truth

Monkfish keep growing all of their lives.

The Naked Mole Rat

Stop by any zoo that has a naked mole rat exhibit and you'll find a crowd happily watching these funny-looking creatures go about their business. These **rodents** are so ugly, they are actually cute!

Naked mole rat

The naked mole rat's name is all wrong. They are not rats or moles. They are actually related to porcupines and guinea pigs. Naked mole rats aren't even naked! These animals have whiskers and some hair on their heads. These hairs help the mole feel its way around in the dark.

Naked mole rats live in hot, dry areas in Africa. They spend almost all of their lives underground. Large colonies of up to 300 rats live in burrows. A naked mole rat burrow can cover as much ground as six football fields! The burrow has many different rooms. Each room has a purpose. Some are used for eating. Other rooms are for giving birth or raising babies. Naked mole rats even have rooms where they go to the bathroom.

The Ugly Truth

Many underground animals are blind. But the naked mole rat can see, although its eyes are very small.

One of the weirdest things about a naked mole rat is its big front teeth. These teeth can move independently. The mole rat can move them back and forth just like a person uses a pair of chopsticks. The mole rat uses its teeth to dig underground. Because its teeth are *outside of its mouth*, it can dig without getting dirt in its mouth!

Naked mole rats live longer than any other rodent. They can live up to 30 years. Scientists are studying naked mole rats to find out why they live so long. Maybe it is their healthy diet. Naked mole rats are herbivores. They eat plant bulbs and roots they find underground.

The Blobfish

The blobfish has an ugly name. However, that name is the perfect description of this ugly animal. A blobfish looks exactly like a blob. It is a soft, lumpy fish that always looks unhappy. However, this ugly creature is really very interesting.

Blobfish live in the waters around Australia and New Zealand. They live 3,000 feet (nearly one km) down at the bottom of the sea. Their squishy bodies have no bones or muscles. Not having any bones or muscles gives the blobfish its blobby appearance. It also allows the creature to float in the water without making any effort. As it floats, it sucks up tiny crabs and other small sea creatures.

In 2013, the blobfish was voted the ugliest animal in the world. The Ugly Animal Preservation Society adopted the blobfish as its mascot. It's true!

The blobfish has no bones or muscle!

If we could see the blobfish at the bottom of the sea, we might not think it was so ugly. That's because the pressure of the water is up to 120 times stronger at the bottom of the sea. That pressure could help the blobfish keep a more **rigid** shape instead of just looking like a blob.

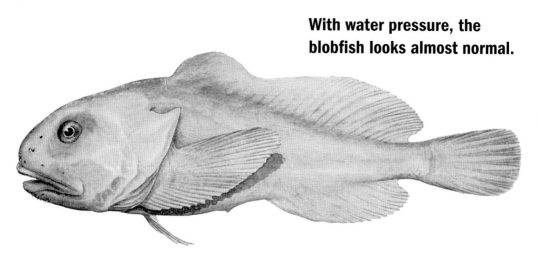

With water pressure, the blobfish looks almost normal.

Female blobfish lay thousands of eggs at the bottom of the ocean. Their eggs are small and pink. The male fertilizes the eggs after they are laid. Either the male or female floats near the eggs to protect them until they hatch.

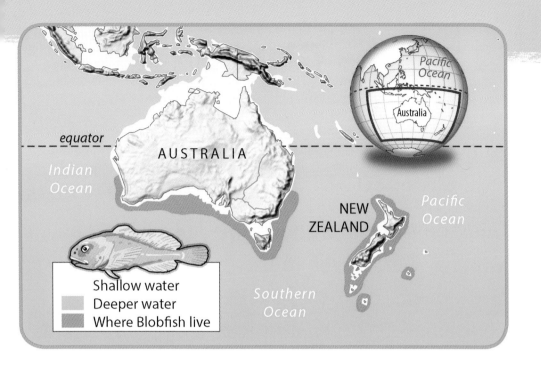

equator

AUSTRALIA

Indian
Ocean

NEW
ZEALAND

Pacific
Ocean

Pacific
Ocean

Australia

Southern
Ocean

Shallow water
Deeper water
Where Blobfish live

Scientists have studied blobfish that have been washed up onshore or caught in fishing nets. Those fishing nets are a big problem for the blobfish. Because there is such a big difference in pressure from the bottom of the sea to the top, the blobfish dies as soon as it comes to the surface. Scientists worry that so many blobfish are killed by fishing nets that this weird-looking creature could soon be endangered.

The Giant Squid

And now, we present the #1 ugliest animal—
THE GIANT SQUID!

Imagine a slimy creature with ten long tentacles,
a lumpy head, eyes in the middle of its body,
and dozens of sticky, sucking disks. That
sounds pretty ugly, and it is! The giant squid
certainly is not the prettiest creature in the sea!

the mantle of
a giant squid

Giant squid up close!

Squids are part of a special group of animals. This group is called **cephalopods**. A cephalopod's head has lots of arms around it. Octopuses have eight arms, while squids have ten. A cephalopod's body is covered by a layer of extra skin called the **mantle**. The mantle works like a bag and holds the animal's organs.

Power Word: cephalopod. *Cephalo* (from Greek Kephale) and *Pod* for foot. A head plus feet.

A squid's body is shaped like a torpedo. It is long and has a pointy head at one end. A squid's eyes are in the middle of its body. Those eyes are huge! A giant squid has the biggest eye of any animal. That eye can be more than 15 inches (38 cm) wide. That's as big around as a soccer ball!

Squids are strange in other ways. Their bodies have two hearts, but they don't have a backbone. They don't have any other bones either! That's why squids have such an ugly, squishy shape.

Having no bones and lots of long arms is good for a squid. These features let the animal squeeze into small spaces. A squid can hide between rocks. There it waits for fish, shrimp, and other small animals to swim by. Those animals might become the squid's dinner.

Probably the most interesting thing about a squid is its arms. They are long and strong, and each arm is lined with two rows of round suckers. A squid's long arms are great for grabbing food. This animal can also pull shells apart by gripping them with its strong suckers. Those suckers also have rows of sharp teeth to grab fish and other prey.

Squids are good swimmers. But they don't swim like fish do! Instead, a squid has a special body part called a **siphon**. The siphon sucks in water Then it pushes the water out. As the water moves out, it propels the squid forward.

The Ugly Truth

A squid's mouth is shaped like a bird's beak. It is so strong, it can cut through a steel cable!

There are many different kinds of squid. As you might have guessed from its name, the giant squid is the largest one of all. These animals can measure up to 60 feet long. That makes the giant squid the largest **invertebrate** in the world!

No one has ever caught a giant squid alive, but scientists have been able to study this huge animal because pieces of it sometimes wash up on beaches. Sometimes fishing boats catch dead squid. Maybe someday a giant squid will be caught alive. Maybe you will be able to see it in an aquarium. Just don't be scared if you come face to face with the world's ugliest animal!

It's difficult to catch giant squid alive.

Ugliest Animal Runners-Up

Here are a few more creatures that didn't quite make the Top 10, but are still pretty ugly!

Aye-aye

Goblin shark

Purple frog

Japanese giant salamander

Hagfish

Glossary

canals waterways built by people to connect two bodies of water

cephalopods animals such as squids or octopuses

endangered in danger of dying out

herbivores animals that only eat plants, no meat

invertebrate an animal without a backbone

mantle extra skin around a cephalopod's body

mascot an animal that is a symbol of a team or group

predators animals that eat other animals for food

prey animals eaten by other animals for food

rigid firm, not flexible or soft

rodents mammals that have large front teeth

savanna a grassy plain in Africa

scavengers animals that eat dead animals for food

siphon something that sucks in water

tentacles long, flexible body parts

tusks long, sharp teeth that stick out of an animal's mouth

Learn More in the Library

You've seen our list of the Top 10 Ugliest Animals and some runners-up as well. Now it's your turn! Are there other animals that you think should be on the list? Go on a search and make your own Top 10 list!

Furstinger, Nancy. *Warthogs* (Animals of Africa), Focus Readers, 2017.

Marsh, Laura. *Ugly Animals*, National Geographic Children's Books, 2017.

Nuzzolo, Deborah. *Hammerhead Sharks*, Capstone Press, 2018.

Index

About the Author

Joanne Mattern is the author of nearly 350 books for children and teens. She began writing when she was a little girl and just never stopped! Joanne loves nonfiction because she enjoys bringing science topics to life and showing young readers that nonfiction is full of compelling stories! Joanne lives in the Hudson Valley of New York State with her husband, four children, and several pets!